F V

St. Louis Community College

Forest Park
Florissant Valley
Meramec

Instructional Resources
St. Louis, Missouri

WOLE SOYINKA

MANDELA'S
E·A·R·T·H
AND OTHER POEMS

"So Now They Burn the Roof Above Her Head," "After the
Deluge," "Appollodorus on the Niger," "The Apotheosis of
Master Sergeant Doe," and "My Tongue Does Not Marry Slogans"
first appeared in *TriQuarterly*, a publication of Northwestern
University.

Library of Congress Cataloging-in-Publication Data

Soyinka, Wole.
    Mandela's earth and other poems.

    I. Title.
PR9387.9.S6M36   1988   821   88-42656
ISBN 0-394-57021-9

Manufactured in the United States of America
24689753
First Edition

Book design by Debbie Glasserman

CONTENTS

ONE

MANDELA'S
E·A·R·T·H

YOUR LOGIC FRIGHTENS ME, MANDELA

Your logic frightens me, Mandela
Your logic frightens me. Those years
Of dreams, of time accelerated in
Visionary hopes, of savoring the task anew,
The call, the tempo primed
To burst in supernovae round a "brave new world"!
Then stillness. Silence. The world closes round
Your sole reality; the rest is . . . dreams?

Your logic frightens me.
How coldly you disdain legerdemains!
"Open Sesame" and—two decades' rust on hinges
Peels at the touch of a conjurer's wand?
White magic, ivory-topped black magic wand,
One moment wand, one moment riot club
Electric cattle prod and whip or *sjambok*
Tearing flesh and spilling blood and brain?

This bag of tricks, whose silk streamers
Turn knotted cords to crush dark temples?
A rabbit punch sneaked beneath the rabbit?
Doves metamorphosed in milk-white talons?
Not for you the olive branch that sprouts
Gun muzzles, barbed-wire garlands, tangled thorns
To wreathe the brows of black, unwilling Christs.

Your patience grows inhuman, Mandela.
Do you grow food? Do you make friends
Of mice and lizards? Measure the growth of grass
For time's unhurried pace?
Are you now the crossword puzzle expert?
Chess? Ah, no! Subversion lurks among
Chess pieces. Structured clash of black and white,
Equal ranged and paced? An equal board? No!
Not on Robben Island. Checkers? Bad to worse.
That game has no respect for class or king-serf
Ordered universe. So, scrabble?

Monopoly? Now, that . . . ! You know
The game's modalities, so do they.
Come collection time, the cards read "White Only"
In the Community Chest. Like a gambler's coin
Both sides heads or tails, the "Chance" cards read:
Go to jail. Go straight to jail. Do not pass "GO".
Do not collect a hundredth rand. Fishes feast,
I think, on those who sought to by-pass "GO"
On Robben Island.

Your logic frightens me, Mandela, your logic
Humbles me. Do you tame geckos?
Do grasshoppers break your silences?
Bats' radar pips pinpoint your statuesque
Gaze transcending distances at will?
Do moths break wing
Against a light bulb's fitful glow

That brings no searing illumination?
Your sight shifts from moth to bulb,
Rests on its pulse-glow fluctuations—
Are kin feelings roused by a broken arc
Of tungsten trapped in vacuum?

Your pulse, I know, has slowed with earth's
Phlegmatic turns. I know your blood
Sagely warms and cools with seasons,
Responds to the lightest breeze
Yet scorns to race with winds (or hurricanes)
That threaten change on tortoise pads.

Is our world light-years away, Mandela?
Lost in visions of that dare supreme
Against a dire supremacy of race,
What brings you back to earth? The night guard's
Inhuman tramp? A sodden eye transgressing through
The Judas hole? Tell me Mandela,
That guard, is he *your* prisoner?

Your bounty threatens me, Mandela, that taut
Drumskin of your heart on which our millions
Dance. I fear we latch, fat leeches
On your veins. Our daily imprecisions
Dull keen edges of your will.
Compromises deplete your act's repletion—
Feeding will-voided stomachs of a continent,
What will be left of you, Mandela?

LIKE RUDOLF HESS, THE MAN SAID!

> *"We keep him (Mandela) for the same reason the Allied*
> *Powers are holding Rudolf Hess."*
> —Pik Botha, South African Foreign Minister

Got you! Trust the Israelis.
I bet they flushed him out, raced him down
From Auschwitz to Durban, and Robben Island.
Mandela? Mandel . . . Mendel . . . Mengel . . . Mengele!
It's he! Nazi superman in sneaky blackface!

A brilliant touch—let's give the devil his due.
Who would seek the Priest of Vivisections
Masquerading as a Black-and-Proud?
No living heart in mouth, one step ahead
Those Jew-vengeance squads.
Safe on Robben Island, paratroops of Zion
Bounty hunters, frogmen, crack Z squads,
Wiesenthal fanatics—here you'll find
Robben Island is no Entebbe. This pogrom maestro
Has his act together—he'll serve time
To spit on borrowed time!

A cunning touch, those modest body counts
In Sharpeville, Soweto. In your heydays,
The crop was tens of thousands. Now who would once
Surmise the mastermind directing death
In tens? Or twenties? Even hundreds!

In your luxurious island home, outfitted
State-of-the-art laboratory, ideas
Flow out to pay the state in kind—protection
For caste research, food for thought.
The ninety-day detention law—your idea?
A ninety-day laboratory per man.
Blackened cells—not padded, no—
You diagnosed inferior minds, not madness. Cells
So lightproof, even the stereotypic eyes
Shed their white pretense—Black is Beautiful?
You made them taste sublimity in Blacked-Out
Solitary.

You listened to their minds go loudly awry.
Mere operational change, from flaying live;
"Improving" on those naïve tries of nature.
Do you feel nostalgia for the past?
Stripping the "circumcised dogs" to buff and
Searching secret parts for jewelry. And your love
For gold teeth—ah yes, gold!
Gassed them cold and questioned their anatomy.
Too bad some woke midsurgery,
But you swung the pendulum the other way
And thousands died from greedy inhalation—
They loved the stuff, they died laughing, no?

Gold! They wore their ransom in their teeth
Their dowry, tithes, death duties. But—

No need *here* for that painful dentistry,
Assaying the yellow fire even before
The body is cold. Our Broederland
Flaunts the gold standard of the world.
Black muscles work it—quickly you adjusted—
None but racial slanderers now predict
A genocide. Modestly you shun the Final Solution—
Who slays the goose that lays such golden eggs?

The gold exposed you. Bloodhound Jews
Whose mouth you quarried for your pay—
Your passion tasting still of blood—
Set their burgled gums to track you down
To the golden tip of the black continent.

Cute Mandgela, sought everywhere,
Cooly ensconced on Robben Island.
I saw your hand in Biko's death, that perfect
Medical scenario, tailormade for you.
And hundreds more of young Icarus syndrome—
Flying suspects, self-propelled
From fifty-story floors
To land on pavements labeled—WHITES ONLY!
You question them only in white preserves—
How would a high-rise building fit in shantytown?

So desperate for acceptance, exhibitionist,
Made omelette of their brains for white

Rights of passage. Sheer sophistry! Skin
Is deep enough. Your lancet Mandgele, was genius,
Creator hand so deft, made anaesthetic
Optional—blue cornea graft, heart-liver swap,
Organic variants—eye in earholes, leg to armpit,
Brain transfer—all child's play to you, but—
Not even you could work a whole-skin graft.
A thousand dead in the attempt
Makes proof enough—wouldn't you say?

Mendgela's in town—the word is passed.
Keep park benches sanitized. White is white
(Though sometimes Jew but—times do change.)—
Black is red is commie menace
Red is what we see when Icarus leaps
A red-forked lightning from cloud-hugging floors,
Tight-lipped, fork-tongued, terror mentors,
Beclouding issues clearly black and white.

And the racial traitors—white Ruth First,
Opens a letter in Harare—*Boom!*—Alibied,
You smile on Robben. Too bad, re colored Brutus,
Mister Boots, Knuckles and Bones. Too athletic?
Caught a bullet but it missed the vital organs
Trying to beat us to the Olympic laurels.
Hassling, hounding Bundbroederland from sports
Our lifeblood, proof of stock and breeding—
Cowards! Like their new uneasy allies—

Those back-stabbing, "trading partners"—
Scared of competition? Of open contest? Right!
We have the carats; keep your plated medals!

Gold! Ah yes, Mandela-Hess,
You got us in this mess. The Allied Powers
Rightly hold you pacing wall to wall,
Treading out your grand designs
In commie jackboots. Mandela-Mengele,
You are *ours*! We'll keep you close.
Your *Doppelgänger* haunts us to the vaults.
Yes, "thars gold in them thar mountains"—would *you*
Let Mandela loose?

SO NOW THEY BURN THE ROOF ABOVE HER HEAD

For Winnie

So now they burn the roof above her head?
Well, what's new? Retarded minds, like infants,
Play with fire. Bright things attract them.
Color obsessed, did not these mewling agents once
Arrest your bedspread?

        It wore, remember,
The colors of the ANC. The patchwork quilt
Inflamed their eyes, dancing in defiance.
They came, they searched, rampaged as only
Red-flag-baited bulls know how. They found
This sheet of love, but hate pursued them.

"My bed, our spread, our bedspread,"
She protested. "A quilt," she taught them,
"By many hands embroidered, it holds
And shares our love, our toil, with all who toil
And share.

"This bedspread knows the pangs of birth.
Like earth in hope of our remaking, it is
Generous in love, a feast
Cast wide to embrace all man and womankind.
Do you wonder then, it wears the hues of hope?

"Love is not lone fulfilled. Embrace
Is gathering-in, the love of man and woman
Leaven in the dough of nation love.
This nest, this rest, this haven from white storms
You raise to thwart homecoming, this battered
Sailcloth mourns the fallen, celebrates
Our rites of passage. Nuptial train and shroud,
Blood stanch or swaddling cloth, desk
And breakfast tray in heat of battle—Foe,
Why marvel it does wear the stripes of strife?

"A standard points the weary feet forward, yet
Wraps the hero's final stillness.
This bedspread cushions us
Against the fall that absence makes."

Still they took her spread away, Mandela
And now they burn the roof above her head.

Nonperson, outlawed of social being,
"Banned." Her image whited out in old group photos
(But who can scrub the mind's retentive plates?)
Her name in blanks, her tongue discolored
By the censor's crayon, they crowed:
"She'll gather mold and time dust, spin
Her censored being in cobwebs of oblivion."
Midmind lies in history's teeth! She was
The rare illuminated scroll in whose prophesies

Humanity discerns its fate. The world would read her
In a hundred tongues.

Whited sepulchers—it is their nature—
Disgorge forgotten leprosies.
Minds in midform, trapped in medieval shrouds,
Their sickness conjured out
Flames of hell, Inquisition's bonfires.
In Winnie they descried all heresiarchs—
Joan of Arc to Salem Seers—frenzied now,
They piled up faggots for the auto-da-fé.

Mammon's Grand Alliances
Begin to crack. The League of Hypocrites
Read the scroll, traceries of fire provide
The dreaded annotations, turn laser heat
To melt the prison bars.

No wonder then, and thus no need to curse
The futile rage, the puny stabs of flames
Disfiguring the night. Death twitches these
Of centuries' buried minds in midformation.
This Witches' Sabbath they invoke will hone
The wooden stake to drive deep through the heart
Of the living dead.

I know they took the spread away, Mandela
And now they burn the roof above her head.

How could they know, these living dead
The flames their fumbling hands have fanned
Inscribe the very colors they proscribe
Across our darkest nights.

FUNERAL SERMON, SOWETO

We wish to bury our dead. Now, a funeral
Is a many-cultured thing. Some races would
Rope a heifer to the slaughter stone, or
Goat/ram/pig or humble cockerel,
Monochrome or striped, spotted, seamless—
The soothsayer rules the aesthetics or,
Rank and circumstance of the dear deceased.
Market rates may ruin devout intentions.
Times austere are known to sanction disrespect,
Spill thinner blood than wished. Still,
Flow it must. Rank tunnels of transition
Must be greased, the bolt of passage loosened,
Home-brewed beer or smuggler's brands, prestigious,
Froth and slosh with ostentation, belch
In discreet bubbles like embarrassed mourners
At the wake. The dead record no disavowal.

We wish to mourn our dead.
Is custom overlooked? No. Our heads
Are shaven clean. Cropped close. Neglected. Matted
Thick with ritual unguents, spiked with clay
Or fiber. Ceremonials well rehearsed,
All outward acts of group cohesion, smothering
Loss, performed. Our headgears bear clan colors.
Portraits, mementos, icons, elders' mats
Laid out in proud parade, mute debts

Of honor, surrogates to vanished breath.
Mummers, griots, play out lineage roles.
The feats, the voices, reverential anecdotes . . .
All to bind us to the "dead but not forgotten."

O dearly beloved, we wish to mourn. But first,
Shall we lance some ancient tumuli? Probe
Some birthly portents, glorified demise?
"When beggars die . . ." You know the verse . . .
But if the heavens launch comets to proclaim
The death of kings, archeological probes
Catalogue our earthly supplement—spent
Rhetoric of skills our earth hoards yield:
Vaults of coins to bribe the other world,
Inlaid bowls, golden lamps, cryptic stellae,
Astral calculus engraved on marble
Mausoleums—the astrologer's final computation?
The jewelled sword hilt, "rich beyond all dreams."
A geography of stasis and cerebral feats
Cheek by jowl across the centuries.
Heliolatrous Incas. Slave and palm oil
Aristocracy on blood-soaked Niger creeks—
Their sportive obsequies arced human skulls,
Fresh-tissued, point to point of silver lances—
Innovative variants of the polo game!
Have we treasures to inter, dear brothers
And sisters? Do we play polo in Soweto?

We wish to bury our dead. Others
Boast horsemen sentinels, ranged in Chinese
Catacombs, silent guards on vanished
Dynasties. Or their Nilotic counterparts—
Did time stand still for these? The labor hours—
Gathering, grading, grinding, mixing,
Mapping the hour of star and moon alignment
To stuff the royal orifice with spices.
Draining toes swelled tuberose with pomp
To ease the slide of rings and golden anklets.
Calf amulets of ivory. Seals on each finger
Equal a nation's ransom. Casque or death mask,
Mines to rival Nature's undiscovered hoards.
Queen, princeling, favorite cat, each
Scrolled in own sarcophagus surround the god-king.
Antechambers lined with lesser beings
Extend the ministry beyond the end
To imagined wants of their lone, lordly dead.

O dearly beloved, seeking solace ever,
Distractions of the mind to ease keen pangs
As we move to bury our dead, we pause only
To contemplate these ancient vanities—
Mongol, Pharaoh, proud Asantehene
All, too lean in frame to fill their grandiose
Subterranean schemes, a troubled sleep
Of ranked retainers swells. Nerveless arms
Redress lost battles, amplify the dream

That thrust a mildewed gauntlet at mortality.
Awesome pyramids on burning sands,
Cunning combs of mind in mountain wombs,
Absentee landlords of necropolis, peopled
By vassals, serfs you dared not leave behind—
How phrased your priests their Final Unction?
Even in death, beware insurrection of life,
And life after debt? Of blood?

We wish to bury our dead. Let all take note,
Our dead were none of these eternal hoarders—
Does the buyer of nothing seek after-sales service?
Not as prophetic intuitions, or sly
Subversive chant do we invoke these ancient
Ghosts, but as that ritual homily
Time-honored in the offices of loss.
Not seeking martyrdom, the midnight knock,
Desecration of our altar, vestments,
Not courting ninety-day detention laws,
The state seal on the voice of man—and God. . . .

We wish only to bury our dead. Shorn
Of all but name, our indelible origin,
For indeed our pride once boasted empires,
Kings and nation builders. Seers. Too soon
The brace of conquest circumscribed our being
Yet found us rooted in that unyielding
Will to life bequeathed from birth, we
Sought no transferred deed of earthly holdings.

Slaves do not possess their kind. Nor do
The truly free.

We wished to bury our dead,
We rendered unto Caesar what was Caesar's.
The right to congregate approved;
Hold procession, eulogize, lament
Procured for a standard fee. All death tariff
Settled in advance, receipted, logged.
A day to cross the barriers of our skin,
Death was accorded purchase rights, a brief license
Subject to withdrawal—we signed acceptance
On the dotted line—"orderly conduct" et cetera.
We now proceed to render earth's to earth.

We wish to mourn our dead. No oil tycoons
We, Mandela, no merchant princes, scions
Of titled lineage. No peerage aspirants
Nor tribal chieftans. Only the shirtless
Ghetto rats that briefly left
The cul-de-sac of hunger, stripes,
Contempt. The same that rose on hind legs
That brief hour in Sharpeville, reddening
The sleepy conscience of the world. We,
The sludge of gold and diamond mines,
Half-chewed morsels of canine sentinels
In nervous chain stores, snow-white parks.
Part-crushed tracks of blinded Saracens,
The butt of hippo trucks, water cannon mush.

We, the bulldozed, twisted shapes of
Shanty lots that mimic black humanity.
Our dead bore no kinship to the race
Of lordly dead, sought no companion dead
To a world they never craved.
We set out to mourn our dead, bugling
No Last Post, no boom of guns in vain salute.

But others donned a deeper indigo than the bereaved.
Unscheduled undertakers spat their lethal dirge
And fifty-eight were sudden bright-attired,
Flung to earth in fake paroxysms of grief.
And then we knew them, counted, laid them out,
Companion voyagers to the dead we mourned.

And now, we wish to bury our dead. . . .

"NO!" HE SAID

(for Nelson Mandela)

Shorn of landmarks, glued to a sere promontory,
The breakers sought to crush his head,
To flush the black will of his race
Back in tidal waves, to flesh-trade centuries,
Bile-slick beyond beachcombing, beyond
Salvage operations but—no, he said.

Sea urchins stung his soul. Albino eels
Searched the cortex of his heart,
His hands thrust high to exorcise
Visions of lost years, slow parade of isolation's
Ghosts. Still they came, seducers of a moment's
Slack in thought, but—no, he said.

And they saw his hands were clenched.
Blood oozed from a thousand pores. A lonely
Fisher tensed against the oilcloth of new dawns,
Hand over hand he hauled. The harvest strained.
Cords turned writhing hawsers in his hands. "Let go!"
The tempters cried, but—no, he said.

Count the passing ships. Whose argosies
Stretch like golden beads on far horizons? Those are
Their present ease, your vanished years. Castaway,
Minnows roost in the hold of that doomed ship

You launched in the eye of storms. Your mast is seaweed
On which pale plankton feed, but—no, he said.

Are you bigger than Nkomati? Blacker
Than hands that signed away a continent for ease?
Lone matador with broken paddle for a lance,
Are you the Horn? The Cape? Sequinned
Constellation of the Bull for tide-tossed
Castaways on pallid sands? No, he said.

The axis of the world has shifted. Even the polar star
Loses its fixity, nudged by man-made planets.
The universe has shrunk. History reechoes as
We plant new space flags of a master race.
You are the afterburn of our crudest launch.
The stars disown you, but—no, he said.

Your tongue is salt swollen, a mute keel
Upended on the seabed of forgotten time.
The present breeds new tasks, same taskmasters.
On that star planet of our galaxy, code-named Bantustan,
They sieve rare diamonds from moon dust. In choice
                                        reserves,
Venerably pastured, you . . . but—no, he said.

That ancient largesse on the mountaintop
Shrinks before our gift's munificence, an offer even
Christ, second-come, could not refuse. Be ebony mascot
On the flagship of our space fleet, still

Through every turbulence, spectator of our Brave New
    World.
Come, Ancient Mariner, but—no, he said—

No! I am no prisoner of this rock, this island,
No ash spew on Milky Ways to conquests old or new.
I am this rock, this island. I toiled,
Precedent on this soil, as in the great dark whale
Of time, Black Hole of the galaxy. Its maw
Turns steel-wrought epochs plankton—yes—and
Vomits out new worlds.

In and out of time warp, I am that rock
In the black hole of the sky.

APOLOGIA *(NKOMATI*)*

Doyen of walls,
Your puzzled frown has spanned the gulf
Between us.
Your stoic pride rejects, I fear,
This homage paid across four thousand miles,
Unfleshed at source, not manifested
In the act. Justice glowers in your rejection—
I submit:

Utterances flung like lead shot will never
Forge the chain mail of our collective will.
Only the salt of sweat-bathed palms
Pressed in anger will corrode
These prison bars. Our caged eagles
Wait on flight, their sweet-stern cry to stir
Our air again. Our assaulted patience
Waits in concert.

We wear our shame like bells on outcasts.
The snail has feet—I know; our jury
Shuffles to assemblage on the feet of snails.
These retreats in face of need

*The Nkomati Accord: put simply, the nonagression pact
    between South Africa and the front-line states.

Betray our being—no wonder
The traitors steep us in contempt!

An old man of sixty-five ekes out his life
In prison slops. The poet
Strings you these lines, Mandela,
To stay from stringing lead.

TWO

AFTER
T · H · E
DELUGE

AFTER THE DELUGE

Once, for a dare,
He filled his heart-shaped swimming pool
With bank notes, high denomination
And fed a pound of caviar to his dog.
The dog was sick; a chartered plane
Flew in replacement for the Persian rug.

He made a billion yen
Leap from Tokyo to Buenos Aires,
Turn somersaults through Brussels,
New York, Sofia and Johannesburg.
It cracked the bullion market open wide.
Governments fell, coalitions cracked
Insurrection raised its bloody flag
From north to south.

He knew his native land through iron gates,
His sight was radar bowls, his hearing
Electronic beams. For flesh and blood,
Kept company with a brace of Dobermans.
But—yes—the worthy causes never lacked
His widow's mite, discreetly publicized.

He escaped the lynch days. He survives.
I dreamt I saw him on a village
Water line, a parched land where

Water is a god
That doles its favors by the drop,
And waiting is a way of life.
Rebellion gleamed yet faintly in his eye
Traversing chrome-and-platinum retreats. There,
Hubs of commerce smoothly turn without
His bidding, and cities where he lately roosted
Have forgotten him, the preying bird
Of passage.

They let him live, but not from pity
Or human sufferance. He scratches life
From earth, no worse a mortal man than the rest.
Far, far away in dreamland splendor,
Creepers twine his gates of bronze relief.
The jade-lined pool is home
To snakes and lizards; they hunt and mate
On crusted algae.

APOLLODORUS ON THE NIGER

—The sale of a continent yet again, in Lagos, during
preparations for the 1977 Black Arts Festival

Apollodorus, merchant-pimp who bore
The wealth of Africa to a barbarian lord,
Rolled artifice in art, a tragic flaw
Disguised to aid the statescraft in the bawd.

Not she dispensed, but took the coated pill.
Cleopatra's needle fell from hands incontinent
While Ceasar's feet stamped patterns of his will
On outspread rugs of an enchanted continent.

There was some poetry alas, Apollodorus, in
Your part, adventurer and alien, beyond
Kith loyalties, pander sublime. Nor sin
Nor history frets against the poet's bond.

Your precedent, Apollodorus is but part heeded
By new black Levantines, purse-ringed, and
    mortgage-beaded.

THE APOTHEOSIS OF MASTER SERGEANT DOE

Welcome, dear Master Sergeant to the fold
Your pace was firm, your passage mean and bold.

Lean your entry, in studied Savior's form
Combat fatigued, self-styled a cleansing storm.

Let other shoulders sprout gold epaulettes
You shunned those status-greedy etiquettes,

Stayed simple Master Sergeant. The nation knew
Who was the Master; the Sergeants rendered due.

The comrade band diminished. The bloody contest played
Its grand finale. Alone the Master planner stayed

The course. The lean had rounded out. The barrack slob,
Close-crop peak-cap head affects new heartthrob

Swinger images. The tie pins are no paste.
The spoils of office, easy acquired taste

Distend the appetite, contract the scruples.
A crow may answer eagle, perched on borrowed steeples.

Flown on flags, graced by diplomatic corps
We consecrate the nightmare, kiss a nation's sore.

To mask the real, the world is turned a stage,
A rampant play of symbols masks a people's rage.

The ass that mimes the Lord's anointed wears
A face that once was human, prone to fears

But crowns are crowns. When rulers meet, their embra
Are of presence. Absent cries make empty phrases.

The pile is high on that red carpet trail
That muffs the steps to your Inaugural Grail,

Skulls like cobbles, bones like harmattan twigs
The squeals of humans dying the death of pigs.

You missed the hisses too; a fanfare covers all.
The whine of violins at the State House Ball

Bears down the whining discords of misrule.
You've proved a grade A pupil from survivors' school.

Your worthy predecessors raise a toast
From exiled havens, or from the eternal roast

Swinging Bokassa, Macias Nguema, Idi Amin Dada
You sucked their teats, you supped from their cannibal
    larder,

And belched in unison. The pinnacle attained,
Next goal is duration. Shall we see you ordained

In the *Guinness Book of Records,* the Master stayer?
Youth is your ally, and appetite of a Master slayer.

Till the people's fiesta: a blood-red streamer
In Monrovian skies, a lamppost and—the swinging
                                                    Redeemer.

Or crisper still: *"Enjoy!"* You feel you'd better!
Buses, subway, park seats push the gospel,
Slogans like tickertapes emblazon foreheads—
"Talk it over with someone—now, not later!"
"Take down fences, not mend them."
"Give a nice smile to someone." But, a tear-duct
Variant: "Have you hugged your child today?"

III. SUBWAY, NEW YORK

I too have dared (and fled) the rage
Of those primordial capsules, rape
Of motion through Manhattan's bowels,
Bronx and Brooklyn, Harlem, Queens,
Rodeo tumbrils plying shallow routes
Through Mammon's sated belly.
Hung on straphangers, shrunk
From defecation smeared as paint—
The drool of ego, fantasies unchained.
"Self-expression" belched the morning
Talk-show pundit, controversial for his pay,
"Safety valve for pent-up violence."
He seeks to place a city's rankness
In its bowels, fool depravity
With permissive cant. I see only
Graffiti violence augmenting decibels
Of snapping strings, tuneless thought.

They are the nation's vocal chords, reels
Of buried tracks shuddering memories to life.
The clang of chain gangs—dead are they?
Forgotten? Perhaps few recognize their ghosts.
The sleek-eyed alley cat on padded feet
That pauses, darts and cleanly savages,
Prepares its feral brew of blood and loot.
Violation is native to its eyes. And fear.
Behind the ego-strut—fear. Each glance,
Resourceful as a blade, invites and stabs.

No, few recognize their ghosts.
Few recognize the time-hatched chickens
"Stomping" home to roost. With every plunge,
With every wombward rip and its unanswered
Scream, remember Bessie Smith. Remember
Muddy Waters, Leadbelly, Sojourner Truth,
Recall that other Railroad Underground,
Remember why the Lady Sang the Blues,
Remember, yes, the Scottsborough Boys,
The sweet-sad death-knell of Joe Hill,
John Brown, and oh, the much-abused,
Misunderstood, sly Uncle Tom.
I saw his patriarch face, at peace,
Reflected in a subway flash. Beside him
An old disguise, snatched at knife point,
From the museum of history's stereotypes.

IV. THE MOST EXPENSIVE ANCHORMAN IN U.S.A.

The most expensive anchorman in U.S.A.
(A million dollars plus per annum after tax)
Hardly ever *reads* the news but, Rather
Makes a news presentation.

A sublime encounter without precedent?
The less time needed to regurgitate
The mush of instant commentary.
Abettors readily on call, by hookup
A button pushed lights up the world's
Despairing ignorance. Banality
Obeys the law of Parkinson, swells
Its reign to fill prime space and time.
The mountain heaves and groans, hems and haws,
Brings forth a Mickey Mouse: Did you note
The President was sweating when he spoke?
Would that be due to camera lights?
Or do we detect a hint of nervousness?
Could we surmise he was not giving all
The facts? Keeping something back? A hint,
A—shall we say—of more disclosures yet
To come? Of course it could be makeup.

"One moment—yes—were you about to say
His tie was knotted just a notch too tight?
He touched it once or twice I noticed. Not tugging,

Just a kind of gentle pat—now that
Could prove a gesture of significance.
I mentioned it in passing to Rick Schram.
You listening Rick? Oh, we lost the picture.
Rick? Ah, there he is. Rick, remember
That new tie of the President? It might
Become the issue, just as I predicted."

The most expensive anchorman in U.S.A.
Rates his sneer a badge of knowing.
Armchair glib, from doughnut mix to spacecraft,
The latest launch postponement earns his scorn.
"Well, there you have it folks—one more delay.
With all the billion-dollar gadgetry,
The most advanced computerworks—it takes
A chance technician with a paper clip
To spot the ten-day glitch. Well, we hold our breath.
Is there a—*latest* forecast? The twelfth I think.
A fuel leak may be the next excuse. Or weather.
Or plumbing problems in the loo. Still
There is always chewing gum to plug a leak—
Let's hope the astronauts are listening—
You listening astronauts? Don't leave home
Without it. And now to something more dependable—
The Bhopal tragedy. With me via satellite
Is Mr. Rajiv Gandhi, Prime Minister
Of India. . . . Rick are you with me?"

The "Go" was given. Postmortem sighed, returned
To school, shed forensic laws to study
Rules of media hype. Science had bowed to gibes,
To wisecracks fueling a nation's expectations.
The O rings lay in wait on mortal hubris. . . .

Mind calloused to universal loss,
Our man declined to blink, stayed squarely
On the ball. The ghoulish game began.
Reruns of fated microseconds, frame by frame
Pandered to a nation's voyeur lust. Kith and kin
The close bereaved were casual anchor fodder.
Master of Ceremonies, cool, unflappable, he
Tortures hours from moments, shakes grief loose
Of cultured silences in humane options.
The understated narrative. Taste
As sometime reticence in dread events.
Our man is jovial host to one more
"Talk show," junk food of wonder palates
In wonderland. The anchor caste rejects
Catharsis. Awe is sentiment. His newsy tongue
Licks the wound anew, bleeds raw bandages.

Rewind. Slow motion. Zoom on frame.
The expert violates the cosmos yet again
Deadsoul questions peel off, robot reel—
"There! That yellow dot. Here it comes in closeup.
Do you see the tiny prick of orange flame?

Would that be the moment of disaster?
Do you think they knew then what was happening?
Let's have a fix on the sequence of events—
We'll turn to NASA—what do you have there, Tom?
You fellows worked out yet the schedule of disaster?
Well, an opinion then. An inspired guess?
What went on within the capsule?—I mean,
The final moments—would you like to comment?
Rather not? Rather not comment?
Now that's unheard of, Rather.

The most expensive anchorman in U.S.A.
Alas, is no exception. A rival station chases
Ratings with a clone—they make a perfect
Koppel. Aliens, still your groans, their viewers
Love them. And strangers may not take their offering
Past the shrine; they'll only feed the faithless.
I plead the pangs of a space nut, self-confessed
Astronaut *manqué;* keep long liquid vigils
Launching day, East or West and nonaligned.
Agonize on every failure, celebrate
The triumphs. I'd volunteer for a voyage
But fear I'll stand accused of my profession
Which tends to the dramatic. Earthbound I remain
Vicarious stowaway on every thrust in space.

The *Challenger* will be replaced. And astronauts.
But not the most expensive anchorman in U.S.A.

V. COLUMBUS CIRCLE, N.Y.

The siren's septic saw edge sheers off
Plate-glass windows, reels off diamond flares
The sun has gouged within their tinted wombs.

A vagrant curses off the lingering fumes
Of last night's laced methyl. Trash cans
Are milestones of his quest, the inns and fields
Of leisured foraging. Contempt replies the stares.

Torsos mimic robots—daybreak, noon break, night
Break kings of dime-and-quarter sidewalks.

Sahel is cool. His wares—tan leather pouches,
Glass and coral, ivory combs and sterile *jigida*
Stake territorial claims. Slit cowrie eyes
Scan approaches for the march of law.

When it rains, the shrewd magician's sack
Transforms exotica to sleek umbrellas,
Guaranteed, in softest rain or breeze—
Auto destruct.

MUHAMMAD ALI AT THE RINGSIDE, 1985

The arena is darkened. A feast of blood
Will follow duly; the spotlights have been borrowed
For a while. These ringside prances
Merely serve to whet the appetite. Gladiators,
Clad tonight in formal mufti, customized,
Milk recognition, savor the night-off, show-off
Rites. Ill fitted in this voyeur company,
The desperate arm wrap of the tiring heart
Gives place to social hugs, the slow count
One to ten to a snappy "Give me five!"
Toothpaste grins replace the death-mask
Rubber gumshield grimaces. Promiscuous
Peck-a-cheek supplants the maestro's peek-a-boo.

The roped arena waits; an umpire tests the floor,
Tests whiplash boundaries of the rope.
The gallant's exhibition rounds possess
These foreplay moments. Gloves in silk-white sheen
Rout lint and leather. Paco Rabanne rules the air.
A tight-arsed soubriette checks her placard smile
To sign the rounds for blood and gore.

Eased from the navel of Bitch-Mother Fame
A microphone, neck-ruffed silver filigree—as one
Who would usurp the victor's garland—stabs the air

For instant prophecies. In cosy insulation, bathed
In teleglow, distant homes have built
Their own vicarious rings—the forecast claimed
Four million viewers on the cable deal alone;
Much "bread" was loaded on the scales
At weighing hour—till scores are settled. One
Will leave the fickle womb tonight
Smeared in combat fluids, a broken fetus.
The other, toned in fire, a dogged phoenix
Oblivious of the slow countdown of inner hurts
Will thrust his leaden fists in air
Night prince of the world of dreams.

One sits still. His silence is a dying count.
At last the lens acknowledges the tested
Hulk that dominates, even in repose
The giddy rounds of furs and diamond pins.
A brief salute—the camera is kind,
Discreetly pans, and masks the doubletalk
Of medicine men—"Has the syndrome
But not the consequence." Promoters, handlers
It's time to throw in the towel—Parkinson's
Polysyllables have failed to tease a rhyme
From the once nimble Louisville Lips.

The camera flees, distressed. But not before
The fire of battle flashes in those eyes
Rekindled by the moment's urge to center stage.

He rules the night space even now, bestrides
The treacherous domain with thighs of bronze,
A dancing mural of delights. Oh Ali! Ale-e-e . . .

What music hurts the massive head tonight, Ali!
The drums, the tin cans, the guitars and *mbira* of Zaire?
Aa-lee! Aa-lee! Aa-lee *Bomaye! Bomaye!*
The Rumble in the Jungle? Beauty and the Beast?
Roll call of Bum-a-Month. The rope-a-dope?
The Thrilla in Manila?—Ah-lee! Ah-lee!
"The closest thing to death," you said. Was that
The greatest, saddest prophesy of all? Oh, Ali!

Black tarantula whose antics hypnotize the foe!
Butterfly sideslipping death from rocket probes.
Bee whose sting, unsheathed, picks the teeth
Of the raging hippopotamus, then fans
The jaw's convergence with its flighty wings.
Needle that threads the snapping fangs
Of crocodiles, knots the tusks of elephants
On rampage. Cricket that claps and chirrups
Round the flailing horn of the rhinoceros,
Then shuffles, does a bugalloo, tap-dances on its tip.
Space that yields, then drowns the intruder
In showers of sparks—oh Ali! Ali!
Esu with faces turned to all four compass points
Astride a weather vane; they sought to trap him,
Slapped the wind each time. He brings a message—
All know the messenger, the neighborhood is roused—

Yet no one sees his face, he waits for no reply,
Only that combination three-four calling card,
The wasp-tail legend: I've been here and gone.
Mortar that goads the pestle: Do you call that
Pounding? The yam is not yet smooth—
Pound, dope, pound! When I have eaten the yam,
I'll chew the fiber that once called itself
A pestle! Warrior who said, "I will not fight,"
And proved a prophet's call to arms against a war.

Cassius Marcellus, Warrior, Muhammad Prophet,
Flesh is clay, all, all too brittle mould.
The bout is over. Frayed and split and autographed,
The gloves are hung up in the Hall of Fame—
Still loaded, even from that first blaze of gold
And glory. Awed multitudes will gaze,
New questers feast on these mementos
And from their shell-shocked remnants
Reinvoke the spell. But the sorcerer is gone,
The lion withdrawn to a lair of time and space
Inaccessible as the sacred lining of a crown
When kings were kings, and lords of rhyme and pace.
The enchantment is over but the spell remains.

MY TONGUE DOES NOT MARRY SLOGANS

For Odia Ofeimun

Sooner plead a writer's block, a cramp,
Akaraba worked by the envious, enchantment
Cast by a beloved siren, jealous of
That constant rival, Muse. Sooner plead
A seven-year dream of leanness, the fat to follow.
Plead a passing inhibition, overdose of reality
That stuns the mind and beggars lyric.
Blame a doctor's caveat on the brain's
Fevered contest with the world. Sooner
Lie in wait than splutter "truths"
Decreed in metronomic swings. "My tongue
Does not readily marry slogans,"
Said the poet. I heard it echo
In the mind's secretive dialogue with itself.
Better a wait in tense silences,
Glimpsing a promise of the future Word,
The poem unsung, the verse that kneads
Abandoned clay, and brings to pulse
The dreamt feast of all humanity.

Rats have gnawed the bloody seals
Off visionary pledges, red-rimed boasts
Moving to the one fulfillment. Only tongues
Questioned in the field of gore dare bring

Advocacy to the sump of blood.
Yet loftiest even of these envisage future
Processes whose means do not demean the end.
The rest is cant, keen cant, the shivering child
That will not come in from cold sleet
Except the house be set ablaze for warmth.
I find no poetry in slaughter fields,
No lyric grace; redemptive passion, no.
Only that which came and went, as others—
The blaze of empires, salvation's ashes,
The crunch of cinders in time's cul-de-sac.
My tongue eschews the doctored mint
Of slogans. Dirge it may,
But not invoke the wake.

Scene:

Multinaira clinics raised to heal.
The shelves stare empty, surgery pans are rusted.
The doctor's reassuring smile replaces
Drugs, his hand prescribes placebos,
Crosses off the hopeless case and
Saves the last pill for a worthier soul. Colonel,
Tycoon, professor, minister, all have vanished
Up the clouds. Their jet will land in Frankfurt,
London, U.S.A., where purring chariots
Waft their bodies to sequestered clinics
Far from madding crowds. These scenarios we know.

Drudge, stay-at-home physician eyes his framed
Hippocratic oath, recalls the other adage:
"Heal thyself," and tranquillizes rage.

Sooner his placebo than its slogan twin.
So, reserve my cross. Till then I will not
Dull our mutual impotence with cant,
Nor stretch the dead end of the place and time
On slogans' half tracks. Nurse,
The placebo that knows itself! Find
A worthier soul for that last, bitter pill.

Empty vials balloon to funeral wreaths
Kwashiorkor bellies stretch to rounded
Water pots and mimic nourishment. No,
There is no poetry yet, but sooner
Silences than tongues that tickle slogans.

Scene:

The bloated victim of a hit-and-run
Ten-day festering. After dinner motorcades
Cruise softly by, stench-proofed
By air-conditioners. Flies buzz the passersby.
A highway patrol pauses, rams oiled gears
For a rapid getaway. Crows hover, patiently.

Scene:

A child's scavenger face, pressed against
A dung heap. Its fingers are inhuman,
Claws regressed to a rooting mammal's
Probe moulting peat, rusted cans and feces.
Onlookers keep a safety space; they think he's cursed,
Not starving.

Scene:

Police checkpoint: "I could shoot you now,"
The lawman screams, and pulls the trigger.
An athlete's brains disperse the pleas
Of good Samaritans. Peacemakers dodge
Gray flakes on motor chassis, paste on arid tar.

You drank in splendor at the watering holes
Of academe, waxed loudly in messianic
Rounds of slogans raised as shields against
Each pleading void. Atavists of Allah
Rose and slit the throats of fellow Moslems,
Screaming, "Mohammed was a slaving Arab."
Ripping thighs off pepper chicken, deftly
Sliding off spiked chunks of skewered *suya,*
You dribbled slogans a thousand safety
Miles away, holding forth by Staff Club
Swimming pools: "These *Maitatsine* only kill

The propertied, the bourgeois parasites,
Fat leeches, Mercedes-owning compradors.
Raise the toast—the revolution has begun!"
The beer foamed white—cost, college subsidized.
Midnight missed you at the barricades
But found you snoring sweetly in your mistress's
Arms, secured by campus walls, manned
Day and night by "wage-slave proletarians."

The ivory towers soar. Skyscrapers race
To register exclusive slogan stakes
On these disputed dunghills—Hear O Hear!—
The record is worn thin, yet the pundit's
Maledictions filter loud, rumbling drum
To surface drum of glazed wall shelters,
Rolling Maorxy-Tongue to Buddha belly:

Because the goal is one, the road is One and no other.
*The footpath shyly prying in toward the road is **not**,*
*Nor **is** a rest in meadows on the way.*
*The scent of rain, the color of night are **not**.*
*The paths of love are not, the fervor of touch is **not**.*
*The clasp of trembling hands on marching knees is **not**,*
*Nor **is** the pause to answer fear or assuage grief—*
(We've censored S.O.S. from letters of the master text.)
*The error of the panicked bow, once drawn, is **not**.*
*The horror of the self-inflicted wound is **not**.*
*The crumbling foothold on the precipice is **not**,*
Nor is the human grasp that faltered at the edge.

*Since **justice** is but One, it must*
Be seized not piecemeal but entire, or not at all,
*And pleas for the moment's justice shall not **be**.*
No more defiant streams of spittle, no,
Not from enfeebled throats whose desperation
*Douses arsonists' flames, for these are **not**.*
The straw-and-wooden ramps by menaced doors,
*Neighbor watched by sleepy eyes are **not**.*
Grass torches flung against the threatened rape
*Are **not**, nor stern exactions when the deed*
Is done. For these are but illusions cast
*To blur **The Goal**. The flawless Destination.*
Alone it makes the one Reality. Not even feces
Smeared on lowly walls and faces, stench
Of agents' power shall earn response
For these are mere diversions, twitches of the End,
*Signposts for knowing prophets of **The Way**.*
*And sores are **not**, and must be left to fester.*
Yaws of undernourishment gouged deeper
*By neglect are **not**, for in their wells*
Deepening ever with pus are glimpsed
Reflections of the distant goal, the One-Cure
Cure-for-All-Eternity of human history.

Oh lotus men, secure in your omniscient Buddha fold,
Clamant heroes of the awaited poem,
There will be random palls of restless victims,
Sprung again to life, against all foreknowledge,

DRAGONFLY AT MY WINDOWPANE

So when I offer me, a medium as
The windowpane, you beat upon it
Frantic wings against unyielding tolerance?

Yet did I envy this, the unambiguous pane
And thought it clarity enough. But you must
War upon it, wings of frosted light,

And charge in thunderclaps? Each dive
Yields proof enough; your parchment shavings read:
Even clarity masks stubborn substance.

And shall this image I present not stay
Its own determined shield? Much dross
Much stone, much jeweled earth and fire

Have fed the stressing of my wall of light.
Let it content you how in me
I yield a stark view of the world, and trust

No inner warp but smudges left
By probing hands, dust of faith-flimsy wings
Distort true vision.

When darkness gathers I may dance
The world in fey reflections; or splay its truths
In a shadow play of doubts.

LOVE POTION

For a Student Believer

Still his hands embrace
Death's kingdom

Love petals from her hair
Turn ashes at the touch

Seeds in dreams alone
Burst this death's withholding

A final mockery floods
Love's winding sheet.

CAMPUS, ILE-IFE

I

When Ogun slammed his anvil down
The flinty earth of Idanre,
Its shock waves burrowed through millenia,
Surfaced in charged outcrops, sinuous
Offsprings, seven-ridged rockhills of Ile-Ife.

II

Their soil serrations read like texts
The sagehood enclave has inscribed
Upon its skin. Gnarled parasites
Retain moss-padded stranglehold
On probing shoots. For these, the sun recedes.
Nature is adept at staging mirrors
Even to the algae's slimy treachery
On rock surfaces. Their oval pools reflect
Horizons slipped askew, settling upside down.

III

The rains of July douse March embers,
Raise frail mists to shroud the gray-flecked
Blackstone of youth's stubborn being.
Cooling vapors lower in vain
On youth's foundations, ambiguous
As cotton flimsies goddesses may don

To ease the passion of fiery hills.
Graceful aging was our prayer but,
Who can rein the restive stallion
On whose flanks the gods have chosen
To make their moist descent!

IV

Stilled are their transit squeaks.
Albino bats will probe in vain
For one familiar echo chamber, scout
Among strange frequencies. At dusk
You made this head your nest, filed
Protest flights across my roof.
Daylight found you, sagging jute bags,
Filled with mush from yet unripened fruits.
Your vampire brothers pass beneath
Sated in unholy suppers of the mind.
They cluster too for safety, but deny it.

CREMATION OF A WORMY CARYATID

Ancient caryatid, too long a host
To woodworms browsing deep within
Your charitable mass, keen mandibles
Have probed your outward piety, aired hidden
Histories through a million perforations.
The borers have worked miracles, lodged
A slow disease within your votive claims.
Their industry, invisible in my gallery gloom
Threads heartwood, hours of skilled devotion
Like spaces of the unknown creative
Hands, now a womb of dust.

Peace, peace, acquisitor heart.
Still your pangs of greed, quit longing,
Douse hunger. Shun furtive middlemen
Assailing Christian, Muslim convertites,
Ministers to aesthetic lust—"Bring out
Your forsaken gods; this agent serves
Paymasters for apostasy." Haggling skills
Contend. Collection rounds end in grimy
Sacks, junk bedfellow with rich rarities.
Then the salivating eye, caressing bronze
And verdigris. Fingertips read wood lore,
Spell chromatic rings that age, sublime
Patina, has glazed as inlaid traceries.

Alas, the mites have punctured hoards of lust,
Left mere form, and scooped the substance.

Wood-be telltale signs, the yellow sift
Of soft collapse alas, departed daily
On conscientious brooms, untutored dusters.
Grand personages—sages, warriors, lords,
And—the ancestor presence too?—remained
Oblivious to their second deaths. Beneath
A sky dome mimicked by a palanquin,
The royal head may hear the din of battle,
Clang of steel on shield, the roaring guns
And screams of courage, death, despair,
But not the thrust of enemies within,
Gnawing entrails of strict hierarchies:

Middle dais—lords and warriors, harem,
Diviners share vicarious power. Lower, the slave
Parade, necks halter-ornamented raw,
Strike plaintive poses on base podium,
Their place and fate among the footstool,
Mortar and pestle, knife and sacrificial rams.
Royalty engrosses all of upper level—
Beads, crown, regal whisk and treasury—
Robes cascading down to rest imperial hem
On tribute bearers, royal feet on headstool.

The ancestral plinth sheers off, obliquely,
From these mortal planes, angled thrust

In sacred isolation, an igneous outcrop
Straining at the bonds of earth.
Bird of swirling plumage, vegetal mask,
It rears at tangent, soughing skyward.
Against the mortal column a demonic lift,
Arbitrating earth and heaven, death and gods.
A ribbed cage veils the inner eye,
Its trail entwines the deeds of living—
Anvil, housepost, cock and corncob—wraps
The cyclic symmetry that ruled the carver's world.

The woodworms' evenhandedness has spared
Neither king nor beast. Lust leaks
From ramhorns, udders ooze their swell.
The fist's salute is palsied; flintlocks trickle
Dust. The stallion's heaving chest caves
Gently inward at a finger's touch.
Heartwood turned porous, time rings finely honed
To render fluid pace to ponderous limbs
Reduced to warts and acne on ancient lacquer.
O Time's aesthetic feast, enslaving eye
And mind; what futile sighs the heart exhales,
Lamenting pliant hands that shaped such heirlooms
Now succumbed to mere mortality.

The mind attunes to loss—a mercy death.
To save the grove, we isolate the tree;
Beyond all cure, uproot, incinerate.
Too ill to grace the backyard rubble, the outcast

Rides the funeral pyre. Yet, the poised hand
Briefly trembles. A passing chord in air,
Mere shard of recollection, a muted
Choral disquiet hovers, plucks at heartstrings,
Pleads a stay of execution. Healthy gods
Alas, disdain weak intercessors. Thumbs
Down-pointed urge the fate of porous caryatids,
Incite the sacrilege with match and kerosene—
Their glories, were they not of fire and sword?

The moment is richly chosen; twilight
Is favorite hour of ancestral parting. I pause
To listen. This music, when it comes
Eschews the drums of marches, trumpets, *kakaki,*
Crests home on herdsmen's flutes of reed,
Gourd xylophones, the *kora's* mournful trills
And distant echoes from dying fields
Of lords of forests, kingdoms long extinct.
Vain to search these airwaves for martial
Rings of glory, rings of anvils at the forge,
Thrust in far horizons. Only their echoes
Linger . . . orphan cries, weightless grains,
Dewdrop rings entwined in spider webs,
Frail bamboo shoots. The ashes' wind sift
In abandoned hearths, grass carbon in bush fires,
Uneasy spirals snared in *gbegbe* leaves . . .

    Mo ja'we gbebe
       I plucked the leaves of *gbegbe*

Ki won ma gbagbe mi
    Lest I be forgotten
Mo ja'we oni tete
    I plucked the leaves of *tete*
Ki won ma te mi mo le
    Lest I be trodden under
Ojo nlo
    The day gently passes
Ko se wa ire
    May it serve us well
Oju ki i mo r'oko r'oko
    The soul adapts to strange lands
Ko gbagbe ile
    Yet ever yearns for home
O ma mi lo ogerere
    And thus, departing, departing,
O ma mi lo ogerere
    And thus, gently departing

The cinders of past epochs sink—but slowly.
Lack of substance clings tenaciously
To form. Pillars rise in flames of conquest,
Peel, incandescent. The reel unwinds
In timeless cycles:
A spearpoint's taper of light.
A head's defiant aureole. Shrine portals
Lower to glowing hearth, back to foundations—
Still they cling to form! Each crumbling
Motion claims new recognition. The equestrian
Loses mount but girds a viaduct's
Evanescent birth. Protean are the stallion's

Shimmering thighs. A cinder ruptures; as fanned
By hot winds, desert blown, the arches sway,
Reform as careful ruins on histories' sands.
Horsemen, groom, lance and standard
Slew half-circle, subsumed in subterranean
Fires. The field of gore glows golden,
Glory-hued to the last hurrah.

Dissolute in the dance of fire, acolytes
Abandon vestments, paraphernalia, soar
Upwards on instant flues, sink back to earth.
Kaleidoscope unflagging, a brace of peacocks
Fan new-hazed triumphal arches where
Slaves in loincloth earlier knelt in homage.
A curtain of flames is parted: glimpsed behind
Shy curtains—solemn brides, immobile gazes
Swivel on lustrous hips, their nuptial dance
Soon shrouded by the falling palanquin. Mortars
Mold superfluous hearths, their pestles
Blacksmiths' tongs for one brief, bellows' breath.

A terse tongue moves to search the ancestral train,
Finned torso of the sacred serpent. It
Finds the inner eye. The explosion
Tears all lingering shards of center plinth,
Brings death grimaces to charred remains
Of slaves and warlords. Each head falls singly,
Each ponderous crash a shore of longing,
Refueling the pool of ash and cinders.

It makes fine ashes. The borers worked well,
Relieved the wood of pith, left flames
An easy core to question. But—the last word
Is of water, as of the beginning;

> Se b'omi ni o pa'na, se b'omi
> > Is it not water that douses fire, is it not
> Ni o pa'na. Se b'omi . . . ?
> > Water that douses fire? Is it not water?

Rain comes as arbiter, *deus ex machina*
Dark horse flexing hooves on roofs of zinc,
Dives to earth, scuffs telltale ashes,
Draws a curtain of discretion on the altar hearth.
This sudden coyness to forestall a second,
Third or fourth idolatory? Urn fetish?
Relic sales? Display of wooden tibia,
Mildly charred, authenticated. Scoops
Of ash in pouches of *egungun* clothing.
Remnant speartip. Halter chip. A cowrie,
Slit intact . . . The intercessor gone,
May mortals not recoup the loss that borers made?

Alas, what's gone is gone. The rain affirms the loss.
Grace that was a fiery dying congeals.
The skies have opened, gods and hero-gods
Blot all traces of their erstwhile dance
With mortals, uphold the lore of pinpricks

Mere woodworms may pronounce on golden realms.
A pottage of ash and cinders marks the spot,
A loathsome mound, pocked by drum throbs
Pressing from the skies. . . . Yes, these stubborn
Scepters, exorcised, yet marrying earth to heaven!